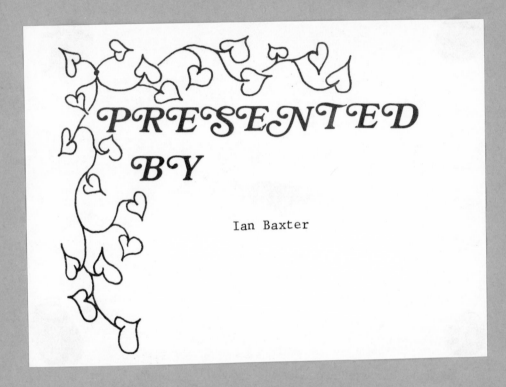

PRESENTED
BY

Ian Baxter

STONE HOUSES
STEPPING STONES FROM THE PAST

Text by Ruth Moffat

Photography by Beverley Bailey Plaxton

The Boston Mills Press

Canadian Cataloguing in Publication Data

Plaxton, Beverley Bailey, 1943-
  Stone houses

Bibliography: p.
ISBN 0-919783-16-3

1. Stone houses — Ontario — History.   I. Moffat,
Ruth, 1942-   II. Title.

FC3062.P57 1984   971.3   C84-099516-4
F1057.8.P57 1984

Title page photo: "The Elder House", Niagara County

Published by:
THE BOSTON MILLS PRESS
98 Main Street
Erin, Ontario N0B 1T0
(519) 833-2407

Winners of the
Heritage Canada
Communications Award

American Association
for State and Local History
Award Winner

Design by Gill Stead

Typeset by Linotext Inc., Toronto
Printed by Friesen Printing Co.

We wish to acknowledge the financial assistance of The Canada Council,
the Ontario Arts Council and the Office of the Secretary of State.

STONE HOUSES

STEPPING STONES FROM THE PAST

"when history is written it becomes a record of the past,
when history is built, it becomes a monument to the past."

The purpose in writing this book was to share our delight in Ontario's heritage of Pre-Confederation stone houses. Although the settlement of Upper Canada has been explored from many angles; we hope our study of old stone houses adds one more facet to an already fascinating history. The houses, themselves, taught us to look a little closer into the past. We are neither historians nor architects but we learned to love these enchanting old homes. Hopefully you will too.

Stone House Index

*For the sake of continuity we have used the term "county" throughout the book, even though many of these counties are now designated as regional municipalities.

CHAPTER I

Of Kings and Queens

"The real essence of early Ontario is found in Loyalist homes and churches along the shores of Lake Ontario from Glengarry to Niagara."

Treasures of Canada

In 1794, the Loyalists arrived in Canada. They settled in what had been, prior to their arrival, immense wilderness. True, Indian trails crisscrossed the forests and furtraders travelled the waterways but there were no civilian settlements. The Loyalists came as refugees bringing almost nothing with them but their determination to remain under British rule. These people had gambled on preserving their property and their rich traditions under the strong protection of the British Empire. They lost everything and had to begin again in Upper Canada. The Crown rewarded them for their loyalty with land grants and some assistance but it was a grim situation which awaited these refugees.

The Loyalist who arrived in Upper Canada and received his land was not necessarily British in origin. Large contingents of German mercenaries had fought for George III and were compensated by the Crown with land in British North America. Some chose to sell their grant and return to Germany but many remained in Upper Canada and formed strong attachments to the province. Settlers of Dutch and Swiss descent were also among those awarded land in Upper Canada. These people had more in common than their loyalty to the British Crown. They were a conservative, hardworking and traditional group. They resisted change and had left their homes, farms and possessions in search of the stability and order offered by the British government. The Loyalists, although not necessarily English in background, believed in the values of the British system.

Although the Loyalists arrived with almost nothing, their dreams of fine homes and farms were not forgotten. As soon as time and circumstances permitted, the loyalist pioneer began to build his permanent home. He built in this new land the same kind of home that he had been forced to leave in the Republic. In the Colonies, he had built in brick or frame; in Upper Canada, stone was there for the taking. It required only the skilled hand of the stonemason to assemble it.

Fortunately, for the Loyalist with the dream of a grander home than his present rude log cabin, there were a few Scottish artisans among the new arrivals to the province. After the disbanding of the Clans in 1745, many Highlanders immigrated to the thirteen Colonies. In 1783, some of these Scots came to Upper Canada with their regiments as Loyalists.[1] Among these Highlanders were the skilled stonemasons that would be so in demand in the new land.

The Loyalist's ideal home was constructed from memory. There were few plans available for domestic dwellings and no trained architects. The builder worked with the client to produce a home that would conform with the owner's remembrance of a traditional Georgian home. It then would be adapted to the needs of the harsher Canadian climate. These "Ontario Georgian" houses had more and larger windows to admit more light into the interiors. They also had more steeply pitched roofs than

their English counterparts. Eventually, sidelights and a fan like transom were added to the traditional Georgian door and this innovation became the "Loyalist door."

The Loyalist was essentially a conservative who preferred the known to the unknown, symmetry to self expression. He had tried to preserve his orderly existence but had lost his bid to keep the Colonies, British. Undaunted, he tackled the wilds of Upper Canada, determined to build the same kind of harmonious life that he had had to leave. The Loyalists admired order and tradition; they respected the status quo. This was reflected in their homes which were tasteful, balanced and substantial. Truly, these Loyalists were the last of the Georgians.[2]

The Manor
PRINCE EDWARD COUNTY

Daniel Reynolds, a young Englishman from the New York colony at Albany, built the first stone house in Upper Canada about 1770. A fur trader by profession and on friendly terms with the Indians, he decided to make his permanent home on the Isle of Quinte. The Indians assisted him in the building of his house by carrying the stone from the limestone ledges of the lake to the nearby building site. Mortar was made by firing limestone over driftwood; this method of stone masonry was no doubt learned by Reynolds from the Dutch builders in his native Albany. "Rubblestone was the favourite building material of the Hudson Valley Dutch. They were thrifty people and it was close at hand."[3] It is fitting that the first house built by a white man in western Upper Canada was built of stone and is still standing today.

The Zwick--Chisholm House

HASTINGS COUNTY

This rubblestone house was built from limestone excavated on the property. John Chisholm was the builder and he sold the house to Captain Philip Zwick. Captain Zwick, an early pioneer of the County, was of Swiss descent. The front door of this house is exceptionally beautiful. Even as early as 1792, there was a formula available to the builders that enabled them to construct perfectly proportioned front doors.

Whitehall

GLENGARRY COUNTY

The 'old country' was in constant need of the tall trees of Upper Canada's vast forests for her shipbuilding industry. The ships' masts were constructed from a single timber. This demand encouraged a booming lumber trade in Canada.

Whitehall was the home of the Campbell family who were involved in the lumber industry. Tradition in the county believes "that some of the dressed (smooth faced) stones found in Glengarry buildings were brought back from Scotland as ballast, after the pine was delivered to Scotland."

Homewood

LEEDS AND GRENVILLE COUNTY

This lovely Georgian home was a reflection of the taste and position of its owner, Doctor Solomon Jones. Doctor, military man, politician businessman, farmer...Solomon Jones pursued life on the frontier with vigour and vision.[4]

In 1800, a growing family and a heightened official capacity in the community made a larger and more imposing house a necessity for Dr. Jones. A Montreal mason, Louis Briere, was commissioned to build a two storey stone house from materials provided by Dr. Jones. The stone for "Homewood" came from the Jones' property. "Homewood" was the work of a French Canadian builder but it was the design and the dream of a United Empire Loyalist who looked to England for his inspiration.

The Ermatinger Old Stone House
ALGOMA COUNTY

Charles Ermatinger was a North West Company fur trader of Swiss background who served with the British Army as a volunteer in the War of 1812. He was part of the force that captured Fort Michilimackinac from the Americans. In 1814, Ermatinger began construction on the stone house which still stands today in Sault Ste. Marie. It is the oldest stone house west of Toronto and in the 1960's was restored to its former impressive state.

The house faces the St. Mary's River and is constructed of split granite fieldstones. It is an immensely strong house with walls thirty inches thick. The stonework is randomly done and the stones are held in place with a lime mortar. There is nothing to indicate the background of the stonemason although Charles Ermatinger was married to the daughter of an Ojibway chief and the Indians in Michigan had been building in stone prior to the arrival of the colonists. It must also be remembered that this location had been the site of a French fur trading post and it is quite possible that the French were responsible for passing on their masonry skills to the new occupants of the trading post. One can only speculate on the origins of the mason who built the Old Stone House in Sault Ste. Marie.

Charles Ermatinger was a justice of the peace for the region and the large stone house served as the social centre for both the local population and all visitors to the district. Those who were entertained at the Ermatingers, spoke in glowing terms of the open handed hospitality that they received in the elegant stone mansion.

Truly an achievement to have access to such Georgian splendour in the wilderness.

The Ermatinger Old Stone House located at the crossroads of East and West has been in the unique position of seeing the history, of not only Upper Canada but of Canada itself, unfold.

The Ermatinger Old Stone House

Mackenzie House

Mackenzie House

NIAGARA COUNTY

This Georgian house, situated in the shadow of Sir Isaac Brock's Monument at Queenston Heights, was abandoned and in ruins when it was rescued by the "job creation program" of the Mackenzie King Government in 1936. It was saved from oblivion because it had served as the home and printing office of William Lyon Mackenzie. He was the radical reformer and fiery editor of the Colonial Advocate. Mackenzie lived in this house for only a year before moving to York; this leaves one to speculate on the background of this house prior to Mackenzie's arrival.

Information regarding the original house is rather scarce and no date as to the exact construction of the house is available. However, it has been stated that when General Sir Isaac Brock was killed during the Battle of Queenston Heights, his body was carried to this house and it lay there for several hours while the battle raged. If this is true, the house would predate the War of 1812-14 by at least several years.

"For many years, the house was only three walls and an inscribed stone. It has been rebuilt from stone quarried from the vicinity to preserve its original characteristics."

The Toronto Telegram   June 18, 1938.

The most outstanding feature of the Georgian home was its entrance. This home is no exception. Georgian doorways were always substantial, complementing the solid traditional nature of their owners. They not only maintained the balance of the exterior but they also indicated the warmth of the welcome that awaited the visitor. The front doors of Georgian houses rarely had door handles as they were usually opened from within. Square or round arched transoms provided light to the interior of the houses. Stone was the ideal medium in which to build these handsome homes; it was as solid and dependable as the men who had had them built.

The Prest--Merritt House

NIAGARA COUNTY

A retired naval sea captain, William Davis built this house which backs onto the escarpment and faces the Niagara River. It was constructed about 1818 of stone from the surrounding fields; the only imported item is the lovely arch for the front doorway. It came by boat from Virginia. This house, although still very Georgian in character, has adapted itself to the condi-tions of the new land. More light is provided by the addition of sidelights and a wider transom to the traditional doorway. This became a feature in the houses of Upper Canada and was known as "The Loyalist Door." The colonists were leaving their own imprint on the domestic architecture of early Ontario.

CHAPTER II

Just Plain Folk

"each ethnic group built houses consistent with their background and traditions."   The American Farmhouse

The Loyalist was not the only colonist disrupted by the War of Independence. The German and Swiss farmers, who had come to the thirteen colonies to escape religious persecution in their own countries, were also placed in jeopardy. Under British rule, they had known peace and prosperity and most importantly, a freedom to pursue their individual religious beliefs. Would the new Republic be as generous? Many of the Plain Folk,[1] as the Mennonites and Quakers came to be called, were apprehensive about maintaining their pacifist religious beliefs under the new government. The American colonists had fought long and hard against their perceived oppressors, the British, and feelings of patriotism were running high in the newly created nation.

"Those that aren't for us, are against us." This statement became a popular slogan among the Americans. The beliefs of the Plain Folk, whether they were Quaker or Mennonite, were totally opposed to this kind of secular commitment. Clearly, the Plain Folk were feeling ill at ease in the militant atmosphere of the United States.

The British Crown in its effort to secure its borders against the new nation welcomed religious minorities to fill the empty lands of Upper Canada. The German speaking Mennonites from Pennsylvania were hardworking excellent farmers. Unlike the Loyalists who had been driven from their homes, the Plain Folk chose to leave. Because they had not fought for the British, they were able to emigrate with money and farm equipment. They required little support from the government. Their only requests were for access to the abundance of good land in Upper Canada and a tolerance for religous freedom. The Mennonites and Quakers were an asset to the small British community establishing itself in Upper Canada.

Although Quaker communities were settled in various regions of Upper Canada, few of the Quakers built their homes in stone. Since access to the fieldstones and limestone was as available to them as to the Mennonite farmers, one must assume that stonemasonry skills were not part of their heritage. The Quakers who came to Upper Canada from the United States were of English and Welsh background.[2]

The Mennonite farmer had a working knowledge of the land. He had not forsaken farming for the attractions of business or the military. His roots were grounded in the soil. He knew instinctively where the best farmland would be located. His ancestors in Germany had farmed on land with a high concentration of limestone and the black walnut tree grew on such soil. When he arrived in Upper Canada, he headed to those areas where there were groves of black walnut trees.[3] He knew then that he had first class soil for farming. Happily, for the future welfare of the young colony, the Loyalist settler learned the German methods of agriculture.

The Mennonites brought with them not only a knowledge of the soil but also a knowledge of stonemasonry. Sturdy stone farmhouses soon dotted the landscape where these Plain Folk settled. The austerity of the Mennonite lifestyle was reflected in their stone homes.

The movement of The Plain Folk into Upper Canada coincided with that of the Loyalists. Their desire to remain neutral in the conflict as well as their desire for religious freedom accounted for their arrival in Upper Canada at much the same time as the Loyalists. Although the Loyalist was the favoured settler, the religious dissenter was not discouraged from settling in the young colony. These hardworking hardy souls were perceived as being beneficial to British North America. The Loyalist had come for political reasons; The Plain Folk came for religious reasons; both groups had a role in the opening up of Upper Canada.

Brubacher House, 1850

Square of Brubacher House from Historical Quilt

The Brubacher House
WATERLOO COUNTY

This solid fieldstone farmhouse was built by John E. Brubacher in 1850. His father, John Brubacher Senior, bought the land for his son, from a Pennsylvanian Mennonite who had subscribed to the German Land Company. The German Land Company was organized in 1803 by a group of Pennsylvania German Mennonites to purchase a large undeveloped tract of land in what was to become Waterloo County.

John E. Brubacher and his wife were the parents of fourteen children. The house that he built is an outstanding example of a Pennsylvania-Georgian or German-Georgian farmhouse, as they came to be called. It combines the exterior features of a Georgian house with the Germanic interior of the Pennsylvania houses. In a traditional Georgian house, the windows flanking the front door would be even in number. In these farmhouses, the front door opened directly into the kitchen area; there was ordinarily only one window on the kitchen side of the front door.[4] The Brubacher house is set on the side of a hill with ground level access to the farmyard. Care and attention to their animals was part of the Mennonite farmer's success in working the land.

The bell on the roof summoned the men working in the fields to their meals; if the bell was rung at any other time, it was a distress signal and the surrounding farmers would react immediately. The Mennonites were a closely knit social as well as religious group and they helped one another in all phases of community life.

This quilted representation of Brubacher House was done by Mrs. Ward Shantz as one of eight squares contained in the Waterloo County Historical Quilt. The quilt was done in 1982 for the Ontario Mennonite Relief Sale and Mrs. Shantz purchased the quilt in honour of her late husband. Today, it hangs in The Erb Street Mennonite Church in Waterloo.

The Holst Farm
WATERLOO COUNTY

Each culture added to the domestic architecture of Upper Canada. The white washed plaster of the front verandah of the Pennsylvania-German farmhouse was an attractive feature of their homes. Their clean bright front porches provided an excellent foil for the variegated colours of the fieldstone walls. The doorways of the German-Georgian houses were not centered; this was in sharp contrast to the symmetrical exterior of the Georgian homes built by the Loyalists. The stone in the Waterloo County farmhomes was not trimmed or squared to any noticeable extent; it was simply removed from the field, placed in the wall and surrounded by a thick band of mortar. The Mennonites were a frugal folk and they employed all the fieldstones with little regard as to size or colour. The end result was far from unpleasant, their farmhouses often resembled patchwork quilts, worked in multi-coloured stones.

The Ellis House
WATERLOO COUNTY

Sam Bricker, a Mennonite from Pennsylvania, was an early settler in Waterloo County. He went back to Pennsylvania to raise the sum of money needed to purchase a large tract of land for those farmers of the Mennonite faith who wished to settle in Canada. While he was waiting for the money to be raised, he spent his time in Pennsylvania learning the techniques of stone masonry. Bricker knew that the fieldstones of the new land could be best employed in building permanent homes for the settlers. He came back to Upper Canada with not only the cash to buy the land but also with the skills needed to construct stone houses. He is credited with building six stone farmhouses in the area, including his own. The Ellis House, built in 1828, is reputed to be one of Sam Bricker's stone houses.

The Break Family Homestead
YORK COUNTY

Waterloo County was not the only area to receive settlers from Pennsylvania. Governor Simcoe had been much impressed by the industry of the Mennonite farmers and he had issued them an invitation to take up land in Upper Canada. This incentive to relocate coincided with the opening up of Yonge Street and York County was the recipient of a number of Mennonite families. The familiar German-Georgian farmhouse with its patchwork masonry and off-centred front door made its appearance in the Markham area. It is highly probable that the Break home originally had a front porch; although the stone exterior was sturdy and resisted the onslaughts of the Canadian climate,

the wooden porches of the early houses often succumbed to the rough usage of weather and time.

Adam Break purchased this lot and the one next to it in 1808. Each lot contained 150 acres and water rights and he paid seventy five pounds for each. The stone farmhouse was built in 1842, in all likelihood, by all or some of his seven sons. Adam Break was listed on the Markham Census of 1861 as being a farmer of Mennonite religious persuasion, who had emigrated from the United States of America. The Mennonites in Pennsylvania were still British citizens and even as late as 1804 were allowed to cross the border into Upper Canada, freely.[5]

CHAPTER III

Monuments from the Military

"The officers of the garrison at Niagara gave a tone to society." Memoirs of Col. John Clark   *"When good military men die, they go to Canada."* King's Men

There is a recurrent theme in the settlement of Upper Canada. From the Loyalist beginnings in 1784 until nationhood in 1867, the British military commanded an enormous influence in the colony. The military was responsible for: choosing the land that would be settled; buying the land from the Indians; surveying and naming the new settlements and reserving land for their loyal Indian friends. They fed, clothed and quartered the thousands of Loyalist refugees who flooded into British North America after the American Revolution. This was not completely altruistic assistance. The foremost goal of the British government was the preservation and advancement of British North America. She could not follow this policy without the presence of strong settlements and a highly visible military force. The British government cared about the settlers in Upper Canada in as much as they formed a line of defense against the newly created United States of America. Her first commitment was to safeguard her British possessions and to this end, healthy, growing settlements were advantageous.

Road building existed not to augment the settlement of the colony but to establish military supply lines. The needs of the settlers came second to the requirements of the British army. Many of the Loyalists, now settled in Upper Canada, were attached to British regiments. They farmed the land but they were always available to defend the young colony. Their direction and leadership came from British officers trained in English military academies. Governor Simcoe, in the short period that he was in Upper Canada, placed a grid of British institutions over the new province, establishing its future as a soundly English province. No matter that its loyalist pioneers were of diverse origins; they would live out their lives under a solid British mantle.

Prior to the War of 1812-14, the strongest influence in the province had been American. It came from the immigrants who had fled the Republic and they were without exception, North American. After the outbreak of hostilities, the American influence in Upper Canada came to an abrupt halt. No longer were colonists from the United States, who wished to capitalize on the wealth of unclaimed land, welcomed in British North America. The British military presence had already been increased as a result of the war and its predominance continued to grow.

A second factor involved in the buildup of the British military influence in Upper Canada was the termination of the Napoleonic Wars and the release of thousands of army and naval men from military duty. There was simply no employment for them in England. Settling them in Upper Canada was an ideal solution. They provided solid British immigration, a ready corps of experienced militia to defend the young colony and once again, Britain was seen to be rewarding her soldiers for their loyalty and service. The British half pay officer became a fixture in Upper Canada. He was an advantaged immigrant in that he was educated, came with his own possessions and more importantly he had an income from his army pension. The retired military man quickly assumed a prominent role in the settling and governing of early Ontario.

The British military provided yet another service to Upper Canada. The officers, trained at smart English military schools, well travelled in their official postings and attuned to the trends of the continent, became the local aristocracy in the province. They provided a sophistication and social awareness that was unavailable to the population from any other source. The garrisons became the focal point of local social activity. An officer gentleman in the Imperial Army was among the best educated of the inhabitants of Upper Canada. His ideas, including his choice of architecture for his home, was much emulated.

In 1811, the Prince of Wales was appointed the Regent for his incapacitated father, George III. This appointment ushered in a new period in the history of the British Empire. The staid symmetry of the Georgian age was no longer in vogue. The Regent, who admired the lightness and elegance of the French court, encouraged this style in all forms of the arts. The resulting architecture, which took its name from the Regent, was transported to Upper Canada by the young army officers who admired the Regent and his innovative style. The Regency cottage became the epitome of elegance for the British officers serving in Canada. "A Regency cottage was generally square in plan, one and a half stories high and with a gently sloping roof. Frequently French doors led to a verandah that encircled the house, so that the beauties of nature could be seen and enjoyed."[1] The Regency cottage, with its spectacular site, was the preferred home for the British military.

The Berthelot House
ESSEX COUNTY

French Canadian settlers were among the earliest white inhabitants of southwestern Ontario. The Berthelot family were merchants from Montreal. Amherstburg or Fort Malden, as it was called then, has long been linked with the British military. The town was in effect, divided in two, half for the soldiers from the fort and half for the townspeople who supplied the fort.

The Berthelot house is located in the civilian part of the town. It was a most satisfactory arrangement for both sides and it is not surprising to find a Regency cottage built for a French Canadian merchant. The fortunes of the fort and the town were intertwined.

Milneholme

HAMILTON-WENTWORTH COUNTY

"Milneholme" in Ancaster had its origins in a military family. This cottage is located on land deeded to Lieutenant William Milne and was probably built by his son. The house displays characteristic Regency features in its simple straight lines, recessed doorway and fewer but larger windows than its predecessors.

Ancaster, located on the Dundas Highway, became important to the new colony after the War of 1812. It was the only community in the Home District with a building still standing that was large enough to hold a court. This area attracted officers, retired from their garrisons, to claim land grants and settle as gentlemen farmers. They did not come to tame the wilderness but to take up residence and hold respected positions in an active growing community.

Stone Shed.

	Purchased.			Made at Penitentiary.		
	£	s.	d.	£	s.	d.
Cast Steel Tools 4cwt., 2q., 13lbs., or 517 lbs. *a* 2s. 4d				60	6	4
Bushards 1 2 23						
Masons and Stone } 2 2 25 } or 496 lbs. *a* 6½d				13	8	8
Cutters Hammers						
Stone Cutter's Mallets .... 112 lbs. *a* 2s. 6d				14	0	0
Lathing Hammers .... 4 *a* 1s. 6d				0	6	0
Masons and Plaisterers Trowels .... 19 *a* 3s. 6d.	3	6	6			
Straight-edges .... 50 *a* 4d				0	16	8
Stone Cutter's Squares .... 37 *a* 2s. 6d				4	12	6
Do Rules .... 30 *a* 10d				1	5	0
12 Water Pails ....*a* 1s. 6d				0	18	0
6 Plumb Lines ....*a* 6d	0	3	0			
4 Mason's Levels *a* 7s 6d, 2 large Squares *a* 3s., 7 Bevels 1s 6d				2	6	6
1 Mason's Line	0	1	0			
736 lbs Tarred Rope ....*a* 11d	33	14	8			
90 lbs. Manilla do ....*a* 9d				3	7	6
Chain .... 1cwt. 1qr. 6lbs ....*a* 6d				3	13	0
500 feet Stone coursers ....*a* 6d				12	10	0
292 " Cut Stone ....*a* 1s 8d				24	6	8
7 Blocks Ornamental do ....*a* 20s				7	0	0
9 " Columns ....*a* 10s				4	10	0
40 Toise Rubble Stone ....*a* 5s				10	0	0
Quarry Picks 2cwt. 3qr. 2lbs. }						
Wedges ...... 0 1 23 }				37	8	0½
Crow Bars ... 4 0 20 } or 1381 lbs. *a* 6½d						
Drills & Sledges 4 4 2 }						
1200 Bushels Road Metal ....*a* 1d				50	0	0

Inventory, Provincial Penitentiary, Kingston, 1840

The Chantry

PRINCE EDWARD COUNTY

The stone for "The Chantry" was cut by prisoners at the Kingston Penitentiary and brought by barge upriver to Prince Edward County. Prison inventories record that the inmates quarried and cut limestone which was then sold to the residents of the province. It is also thought that some stone masons learned their trade while serving their sentences at the Penitentiary. They then returned to society and practised their newly acquired skills in building stone homes in Upper Canada.

Ballyhill House
The William G. Howes House
PRINCE EDWARD COUNTY

Location was as much a part of the Regency architecture as the house itself. This house located on a height of land overlooking the lake is no exception. Regency taste declared that all aspects of a house be congruent. The windows in these houses commanded as much attention as the door. Verandahs became a popular feature of the Regency house; the owners in their military postings were well travelled and brought to their new homes ideas which they had seen in other lands.

Backview of Ballyhill House

These early homes often predated the arrival of roads, travel in Upper Canada being customarily by water. It became difficult for the owner to decide where to locate the front of the house. The builder of Ballyhill House resolved this problem in a neat fashion by having two attractive facades. Either one would have presented a most agreeable face to this enchanting Regency house.

Barberry Cottage

Barberry Cottage

FRONTENAC COUNTY

After the War of 1812, Kingston became the gateway to a rapidly developing province. The presence of the military stimulated the commercial growth of the city. Fort Henry and the dockyards at Barriefield utilized stonemasons in the building of their military installations. When the masons had completed their work for the British Army, they were free to find employment in building homes for the swelling population of Kingston. The War of 1812 had given a sharp stimulus to the growth of the town and the demand for housing was increasing. The construction of houses from stone was an obvious choice for those wishing to live in Kingston. There was an abundance of easily quarried limestone available in the area.

This lovely Regency house was built for the Lieutenant-Governor of the province in 1841, when Kingston had been chosen as the capital of Upper and Lower Canada. However, His Excellency never occupied this residence as the status of Kingston as the capital of Canada was of such short duration. The house was called "Barberry Cottage" after the Scottish tradition of naming a house for the plants that grew in its garden. Large French doors leading to a wide verandah attest to the military influence in this Regency cottage built of local limestone.

Riverest

Riverest

PRESCOTT AND RUSSELL COUNTY

On the banks of the Ottawa River is Riverest, an exquisite Regency house built in 1833. Its picturesque site with large lawns and high hedges creates a wonderful setting for this stone cottage. In keeping with the dictates of Regency taste, "all things having equal worth," not only the doors but also the windows of Riverest have sidelights and a fan transom. An ornate verandah and decorative chimneys complete the exterior of this classic Regency cottage. It has been suggested that Army engineers who were building a dam nearby were responsible for the construction of Riverest.

When the half pay officers located on land where stone was readily available, the Regency cottage, executed in stone, was built. They are the monuments to the military in Upper Canada.

Construction of the Fisher House

Completion of the Fisher House

*Photographs courtesy of Mrs. M. Fisher,
Cambridge, Ontario*

CHAPTER IV

Sticks and Stones

"Mixed fieldstones, scattered everywhere by retreating glaciers, were split and squared and used extensively in building farmhouses."

Our Heritage in Stone

The building of stone houses in Upper Canada was never undertaken haphazardly. The settler's first dwelling was a log cabin; the materials and skills needed to construct it were available to all but the most inexperienced of pioneers. His next dwelling was his first real home. Something went into these homes that was beyond mere shelter. The stone house was built deliberately and was built to last. It isn't by chance that so many of our early stone houses have survived the passage of time. The settler's stone farmhouse was his commitment to his new land. He meant to stay.

It wasn't enough that he merely wished to establish his permanence in Upper Canada. He had to find the materials to build his house. Fortunately, for the settlers there was an abundance of stone readily available. Outcrops of limestone appear in the eastern portions of the province as well as in the Niagara Escarpment. There were other deposits where rivers had worn away the topsoil and left the limestone exposed. Fieldstone boulders remained in the newly cleared fields of the early settlers. They had been deposited by the retreating glaciers of the early Ice Age. The stone was close at hand and the settlers did not have to transport it any great distance.

"There were no experienced stonemasons among the loyalist refugees, who arrived after the American Revolutionary War, except some of Dutch-German origin who came from Pennsylvania or the Hudson River Valley. In the United States, prior to 1800, buildings had been almost exclusively of wood or brick construction."[1]

That did not exclude all stone construction in Upper Canada in that period. It simply suggests that the colonists were restricted in their choice of building materials by the lack of skilled stonemasons available at this time. In Lower Canada, the French had been building in stone for over a century. They had many fine masons. For the Loyalist of means, a stonemason could be hired from Quebec. "Homewood" at Maitland, Ontario is a fine example of a Georgian home built by a French stonemason. Stonemasons came to Upper Canada in numbers after 1827. Economic circumstances dictated their arrival. The building of the Rideau Canal required the specialized skills of the stone mason; there were not sufficient numbers of masons in the colony to undertake such a mammoth project. Recruiting took place in Scotland at a time when the country was experiencing a dire depression. The stonemasons came, built the canal and stayed in Upper Canada. They moved from east to west, building stone houses wherever there was a demand. They were professionals with a marketable skill and they travelled far from their home communities in the execution of their work.

The mason and the material were now present in Upper Canada. The construction of stone houses in numbers was now possible.

The Stone Yard

Photographs courtesy of the
Archives of Ontario

A Plug and Feathers

Marks in Stone where it was Split

The Upper Canadian stone mason did not have a wide assortment of tools at his disposal. He had to be very creative in his management of these heavy stones. Plugs and feathers were used in splitting the stone; stone boats transported the boulders from the fields. A hammer and a chisel were the available tools for trimming the stones and giving the window and door openings a decorative finished appearance.

The rubble stone wall was really two walls, an inner and an outer wall; it was held together with "tie stones" which stretched between both walls. The space between the two walls was filled with leftover bits of stone and mortar. The master mason would work on the exterior wall while his apprentice worked on the inside wall.

The construction of a stone house required a great many labourers. It took many men, months and even years to complete the building of a stone house.

Exposed interior of a Stone Wall

Cobblestone Construction
Levi Boughton, a mason from Albany, New York, brought this specialized stonework to Paris, Ontario. It remained in Paris, a local phenomenon.

Stone Masonry Styles

Parging
The French Canadian masons smeared the mortar, so that only a small portion of each stone was visible. This method of applying mortar was originally called pargeting.

Patchwork Construction
The stonemasons with a German background placed the stones randomly, with little regard for size or colour. Thick bands of mortar held the stones in place.

Mortar
Although the stone in this wall is quite gray, the overall appearance of the masonry wall is that of a warm yellow hue. The colour of the mortar has given its own tones to the house.

Coursing
The Scottish masons had a penchant for straight rows (courses) and narrow bands of mortar. This gave the stone walls a clean appearance with an emphasis on the stones themselves.

Plaster of Paris
The mortar in this wall has been coated with plaster of Paris. The masons were constantly searching for methods of weatherproofing their work.

A Cambridge Cottage of Blue-Grey Stone

WATERLOO COUNTY

The stone for these Ontario cottages came in various colours and compositions. It ranged from the hard blue white of the Kingston area to the dark gray of the eastern counties. In the Grand River Valley, the stone might have a warm beige hue or the blue-black glitter of granite. In Leeds County, a dark yellow colour appears in the stone, while in Credit River stone, pink is the predominant shade.

The stone masons themselves employed the colours of the stone to add another dimension to the house and to their craft. Comments concerning the look of a stone house circulated among the local population.

"Pink stones make prettier walls."

"Black stones should be placed near the bottom of a wall because too much black in the stones makes a house frown." [2]

The East Wing of Thistle Ha' Farm
DURHAM COUNTY

John Miller, the original owner of this large farmhouse, was a Scotsman but he hired two Yorkshiremen to build his stone house. He paid them one dollar and twenty five cents per day for their work. They were highly skilled craftsmen who were much in demand. The stone for Thistle Ha' came from the fields surrounding the farm and it took three men working for two years to split and trim the stone used in building the house.

The name of the house reflects its owner's Scottish origins, the thistle, being the national emblem of Scotland and Ha' meaning smaller than a Hall. The farmhouse was far from being small by Upper Canadian standards, in that it boasted a ballroom in its east wing.

*INVOICE OF GOODS SENT TO CHARLES OAKES ERMATINGER AT SAULT STE. MARIE
VIA LACHINE IN MAY 1821 INCLUDED THE FOLLOWING:*

4 boxes Window Glass, 8½ x 9½

3 Smith's Hammers and 4 Mason's Hammers

4 Mason's trowels

2 Plaister's trowels

1 –three-foot (Three ovens) double stove

1 Ash pan for stove

2 10-m stock locks

4 9-m stock locks

1 Metal tea pot

1 Pad Lock

1 cut glass mustard pot

1 cut glass Vinegar Cruet

1 cut glass Pepper shaker

1 cut glass Salt shaker

1 Inkstand, plated top

2 doz. Table tumblers

2 Pairs—quart decanters.

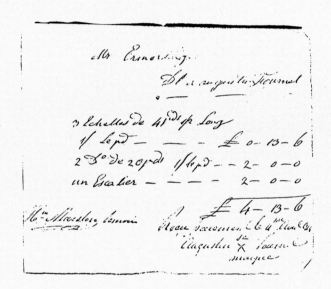

The settlers of Upper Canada, when they became sufficiently affluent, sent to Montreal for the items they wished to have in their homes. Montreal was the centre of commerce for the Canadas and luxury goods were imported from England and the continent.

Courtesy of The Ermatinger Old Stone House Museum. (see page 14)

The Jackson House

LANARK COUNTY

The appearance of a door in the gable of the Ontario cottage gave rise to wonderful stories concerning its function. The existence of the "suicide door" can be accounted for in one of two explanations. Either the owner did not wish to finish the verandah in order to delay the arrival of the tax collector, or time and weather combined to contribute to the demise of the original wooden structure which was never replaced. Neither explanation makes for a good story.

The windows in The Jackson House are three panes in width, dating the house to 1835. By this date, it was possible to have glass made in this size. Prior to 1835, four or five panes were necessary to complete the width of the window. The double hung windows were of Dutch origin and came to Upper Canada via England. They were particularly welcome in Canada in that they admitted ample light while restricting cold drafts into the interior of the house.

The Bruner Farmhouse
ESSEX COUNTY

This farmhouse was built in 1863 of fieldstone cleared from the surrounding land; the white clapboard portion is a turn of the century addition. The board running under the upper windows and the one running above the front door indicate where the porch was attached to the house. It was supported by stone posts which are still in place. This architecture, in which the gabled end of the house forms the front, was the only one in stone that we found. The Bruner family came to this area from Pennsylvania and perhaps, the origin of this house design had its roots there.

The Jasper Golden House
ESSEX COUNTY

Extensive renovations have been done to this stone cottage to enable the descendants of the Golden family to live there today. This house has no foundation. It was built on top of fieldstone boulders. The large limestone cornerstones were said to have been brought as ballast by boat from Niagara. Limestone is much easier to square and trim than the granite of fieldstone.

A Farmhouse at Crosshill

WATERLOO COUNTY

This fieldstone farmhouse owes its distinction to the exquisite patterning achieved in the stonework by an expert craftsman. The colours and sizes of the stones were placed according to a scheme known only to the stonemason and executed only by him. The side walls of this house, although beautifully done, do not exhibit the same attention to patterning as does the front wall of the house. An apprentice may well have been responsible for the work on the side walls.

Ruined Stone House

LEEDS AND GRENVILLE COUNTY

Each mason had his own formula for making mortar. Basically, the method used was to burn timber and limestone fragments until it was a fine ash. This ash was mixed with water and sand to produce the mortar for the stonework. The quality of the mortar determined the longevity of the house. If the mortar did not stand the test of time and weather, the stone simply fell from the walls. The mortar had to be somewhat soft to allow the stone to move without breaking the mortar and yet it had to be strong enough to resist the severe Canadian climate. Finding a formula to suit these conditions was a formidable test for any stonemason. Some masons slanted the mortar out to allow the rain to slide off, while others coated their mortar with plaster of Paris to weatherproof their work. Grit was the term used to describe the kind of first grade sand the Scottish stonemasons used in making mortar.[*3]

[*]Alexander Mackenzie, a Scottish stonemason was the first Liberal Prime Minister of Canada. It was appropriate that the popular name for his party came from his profession.

Inge-Va

LANARK COUNTY

This stone house was built in 1824 by the Rev. Michael Harris, the first Anglican minister in Perth, Ontario. He had also served as Ensign Harris in the War of 1812 and saw action in the Niagara region. The house was built of local sandstone by Scottish stonemasons who had settled in the area. Originally the house did not have a peak and bore a resemblance to the stone houses of Rev. Harris' native Ireland.

CHAPTER V

Stone in the Vernacular

"stone houses soon superceded log cabins." Canadian Geographical Journal, 1949

Milestones in the Rideau-Ottawa Valley

In 1815 the British government ever mindful of the danger to the south of Upper Canada instituted a policy of Military Settlements.

This policy had a twofold aim: to establish a loyal population inland and to provide an alternate route for the transportation of men and supplies into the Upper Province, away from the exposed shores of the St. Lawrence River. A population safely tucked in the backwoods of the colony could supply goods to those on active duty. An interior waterway system was deemed a necessity by the military staff in Upper Canada. The young colony had had a close call in the War of 1812-14 and those responsible for the survival of British North America were determined to do everything possible to ensure its future safety.

Conditions in Britain at this time were particularly depressing for the working classes and immigration to Canada had a great appeal; especially as the British government undertook to offer assistance to those wishing to emigrate.

"On February 22, 1815, a Proclamation was published at Edinburgh, which set forth the government's plan."[1] The settlement at Perth was comprised of Scottish immigrants looking for a better life and governed by British officers, dedicated to defending Upper Canada from the encroachment of the Americans.

Although the need for the building of an inland supply route was recognized by the military in 1815, the actual construction of the Rideau Canal did not begin until 1826. It was at this time that the call went out for stonemasons to build the canal. There were not sufficient numbers of masons in Upper Canada to complete this massive military project. The promise of employment with good pay brought an immediate response from the skilled stonemasons of Scotland. When the work on the canal was finished in 1834, they did not return to Scotland. The lasting imprint of these Scottish masons was not in the Rideau Canal, which never had to serve the function for which it was built but in the stone houses that dot the countryside of the Rideau-Ottawa Valley.

The Joyce House
FRONTENAC COUNTY

The Ontario Cottage, a one or one and a half storey house, started with Georgian styling and then reflected Loyalist adaptations. A gable over the front door was often added to allow more light into the loft. This gable became a trademark of the province. The Ontario Cottage, a uniquely Upper Canadian building style, was executed in both the Eastern and Western regions of the province by Scottish stonemasons who shared a common heritage.

A Rideau Valley Cottage

LEEDS AND GRENVILLE COUNTY

The George Merrick House, 1840.
A Loyalist Cottage

The Stephen Merrick House, 1844.
A Classical Revival House

The Merrick Houses

LANARK COUNTY

The founder of Merrickville, William Merrick, had three sons who built three stone houses.

The Aaron Merrick House, 1845.
A Georgian Manor

Milestones in the Grand River Valley

"The city of Perth on the River Tay is to the southeastern section of Ontario what Guelph is to the west, the heart of a vast district of Scottish settlement.[2]

At approximately the same time as the masons from the Rideau Valley were released from canal building, Scottish land agents were busy purchasing land in the Grand River Valley and the Huron Tract. These men sold the land to Scottish settlers who were seeking to escape the abject poverty of their lives in the old country. The settlers brought with them their stone-masonry skills and it was not long before their original log cabins were replaced by neat stone cottages, expertly crafted. As the province grew, so did the numbers of stone houses for now there was an ample supply of stonemasons among the local population. The completion of a stone house became a milestone in the life of a pioneer family. It anchored their relationship to the new country.

This period 1836-1860 was the heyday of prosperity and building in Upper Canada. Queen Victoria was on the throne; peace seemed to be lasting and the resulting stability provided an atmosphere of well being to the province. It was in this period that many stone "Ontario Cottages" were completed. The coming of the railway to Upper Canada spelt the demise of the small stone house. As a generation earlier had been lured with the promise of good wages to the building of the canal, the next generation was attracted to the building of the railways with the same promise. Once again, the departure of the cheap labour put the building of stone houses out of reach of all but the wealthy.

Ontario Cottages
in the Grand River Valley
WATERLOO COUNTY

A chimney perched on the gable of the Ontario Cottage indicated the presence of a hall stove with its attendant pipes. By 1840 the residents of Upper Canada were moving from the pioneer period into a more comfortable existence.

The Old McLean House
WELLINGTON COUNTY

Hamilton House

BRANT COUNTY

The Cobblestone Era began in New York State with the completion of the Erie Canal. The stone masons were then free to build houses; they put their skills to work with the cobblestones that were available from the lakes and fields. These houses of cobblestone masonry were amazingly durable, requiring no painting or weatherproofing, but they took many men, hundreds of hours, to complete. The entire family helped in the construction of a cobblestone house. The job of the old and the young was to sort the stones according to size, shape and colour. The stones were then stacked lengthwise to form the wall with the exposed end of each stone forming the cobblestone.

This cobblestone house is the most noteworthy of the houses that Levi Boughton built. It took five years to complete and one mason worked all day to finish two courses (rows) of the long side of this house. Adding to an already grand exterior is the belvedere; this glassed enclosure gave exceptional light to the second storey. Hamilton House was completed in 1844.

Deans Farm

BRANT COUNTY

At the opposite end of the cobblestone architecture is the simple farmhouse of the Deans family. It is believed that Levi Boughton started the building of this house because the first five courses bear his trademark. He placed the stones on a slight angle. The house was probably finished by one of his apprentices.

CHAPTER VI

Hearthstones
The Stone Farmhouses of Upper Canada

The Four All's
First came the King, who owned all
Second came the parson, who prayed for all
Third came the soldier, who fought for all
and lastly, the backbone of Canada, then as now
the farmer with his plough, who paid all.

History of Weston

The Cameron Farm
YORK COUNTY

Flora Cameron, a Scottish widow, had this house built for her in the same year that Tara was built. This was an era of extensive stone house construction. Folklore tells us that the front steps on these stone farmhouses were often not built until the first daughter was to be married. The taxman in those days did not come to collect his taxes until the new house was finished. In many Scottish homes, the front steps took a long time to complete.

Tara
The Andrew and Zephera Wilson House
DUFFERIN COUNTY

The Conlins, an Irish family, received their land grant in 1833. They built their stone farmhouse in 1858. It has been noted that the house resembles an Irish manse. All the material came from the farm property and a stone mason from nearby Fergus was probably engaged to do the masonry. It is reputed to have cost twelve hundred dollars to build. In many of the farmhouses, a coin was placed somewhere in the building by the mason as a record of the year that the house was finished.

The Stirling House
YORK COUNTY

The stone mason who built the Stirling house in 1860 was called Nathan Jackson. He is credited with building three other houses in the area. This house has a definite pattern in black and white stone and the cornerstones and lintels (door and window openings) are of Kingston limestone. The Scarborough area is rich in old stone houses, due to the abundance of granite fieldstones left by the retreating glacier and to the Scottish background of her early settlers.

Courtesy R. Schofield Collection

The Horsley Farm

YORK COUNTY

The discovery of stone farmhouses with red brick trim in parts of York County raised a question. Why was brick used instead of stone to form the lintels (the top support for a window or door opening) and cornerstones of some of the houses in this area? The answer probably lies in the realm of finance.

Imported Kingston limestone was costly; locally made brick was inexpensive. Those farmers who could afford to, purchased the smooth, easily dressed Kingston limestone for their quoins (cornerstones) and window trim; the rest used the red brick of the area. The Upper Canadian farmer was nothing if not inventive.

Zimmerberg

WELLINGTON COUNTY

The story is told, that the Scottish stonemason who built this substantial farmhouse cut, squared, faced and trimmed the front wall of the house for free. It was a demonstration of his ability as a stonemason. The theory being, if the prospective client liked his work, the mason was then hired to build the house. The front of the house was the most important to the owner and if the stone mason could do a superior job on the front wall, then he would certainly be capable of doing the rest of the stone-work, as it required a lesser degree of skill. The sides and backs of many of the stone houses were pieced together from the ends left over from the squaring and trimming process used to give the front of the house its imposing appearance. This "rubble-stone" was the Scottish masons' way of utilizing all of the stone in the building of a house. These houses were said to have "a Lady Anne front and a Maryann back."

The Old House

GLENGARRY COUNTY

The neat appearance of the storey and a half cottage in Upper Canada had its origins in the early tax structure of the province. Houses with two stories or more were subject to extra taxation. Arthur Cameron built this stone cottage in 1853. His initials and the date are carved in the keystone over the front door.

Kinhaven Farm

GLENGARRY COUNTY

The Kinloch brothers of Scotland were brought to Upper Canada to build a stone church for the Highland Scots of Glengarry. Upon its completion, one of the brothers went to Montreal where he found employment as a stonemason working on such notable buildings as St. James Cathedral and the Bonsecours Market. He returned to Glengarry County in 1849 and began to build the stone farmhouse that still shelters his descendants today.

The appearance of Kinhaven Farm suggests a French Canadian influence in its slightly bell shaped roof and the extended eaves over a narrow porch. The skill of the master mason is most apparent in the exceptional stonework surrounding the doors and windows.[1]

The Palmer House
PRINCE EDWARD COUNTY

Built between 1840 and 1850, this stone farmhouse features a lantern to light its second storey. One problem, common to all homebuilders in Upper Canada, was to find ways to let sufficient daylight into the interiors of their houses without letting the cold in at the same time. Our long dark Canadian winters accentuated the need to provide as much light as possible. Each building era offered its own solution. The Georgian houses had transoms over their entrance doors; the Loyalist homes had wider transoms and sidelights surrounding their doorways; the Regency builders moved the emphasis on light away from the entrance, installing large French doors in place of the smaller windows. The Ontario cottage had a gable over the front entrance with a window in it to provide light to the upper floor. By far the most entrancing solution to the light problem was the installation of a belvedere (a glassed in room on the crown of the roof) or a lantern (windows set on the crest of the roof.) In effect, these structures were Upper Canadian skylights.

Fairview

CHAPTER VII

Cornerstones of the Community

"This house reflects a sense of prosperity, permanency and solidity."
The Guide Book, Upper Canada Village

By the middle of the nineteenth century, residents in Upper Canada were no longer in pioneer settlements. They had established farms and businesses in functioning communities. The frontier had disappeared from the province and had moved further west. The citizens of the country required the services provided by a stable and responsible government. The threat of invasion from the United States had, by this time, faded and Upper Canadians were anxious to get on with the business of nation building.

Doctors had an important role to play in their communities not only as healers but also as justices of the peace. There was a shortage of educated men in the province and those who knew how to read and write had to assume more responsibility for the routine services that the citizenry wished provided. The same held true for the clergyman. He was no longer an itinerant minister preaching to a scattered flock; he was now an esteemed member of society with a permanent church in an established parish.

Fairview
HAMILTON–WENTWORTH COUNTY

This imposing home located on a rise of land once thick with black walnut trees was owned by the local doctor. Dr. Farmer administered to his patients from the circular, windowed room at the west end of the house, known as the surgery. The stone for all three houses pictured in the aerial photograph came from the now water filled quarry. "Fairview" is located at the top of the photograph.

Pinegrove

LEEDS AND GRENVILLE COUNTY

The gracious home of the Rev. Dr. Robert Blakey, the first
resident minister of the Blue Church, was built in 1822 on the
banks of the St. Lawrence River near Prescott.

The Stone Manse

GLENGARRY COUNTY

The Kinloch brothers are credited with building this stone house at Martintown about 1830. The rounded dormer windows are unique but the stonework is not as fine as that of the Kinloch farmhouse built some twenty years later. The masonry skills of Alexander Kinloch were obviously polished by his years of experience in Montreal.

Hutchison House
PETERBOROUGH COUNTY

Dr. John Hutchison, a skilled surgeon with a young growing family, was considering leaving his practice in Peterborough for the urbanity of Toronto. When the local citizens heard this, they decided to build him a fine stone house as an inducement to remain in Peterborough. The entire community co-operated in the construction of the Doctor's house. Their strategy worked, Dr. Hutchison and his family remained in Peterborough until his death a few years later.

This was an era of unbridled economic activity and businesses flourished. The railway was coming to Upper Canada with its promise of easy accessibility to new markets. As the province blossomed so did the middle class. Merchants, mill-owners, bankers, farmers, all were free to participate in the growth of Upper Canada.

These men were the leaders of their respective communities and required homes that reflected their special status. Stone, where masons and material were available, was the ideal medium in which to build. Strength and permanence, inherent qualities of stone, were the perception that this society had of its leading citizens. Most professionals worked from their homes and they needed an imposing and efficient residence. Their stone houses gave substance not only to the person but also to his profession.

The Alpheus Jones House

LEEDS AND GRENVILLE COUNTY

This beautifully built stone house, set in parklike surroundings, was the home of Prescott's first postmaster. Alpheus Jones was also the first customs collector in Prescott. In the early 19th century, Prescott served as an important center for Upper Canada. It had a natural deep water harbour and as such was the depot for both goods coming into the interior and for the great timbers leaving Upper Canada, destined for the shipbuilding yards of Britain.

The McIntosh Stone Cottage
PERTH COUNTY

The original owner of this restored stone cottage was mill-owner, Gilbert McIntosh. The mills and the limestone quarries of St. Marys employed the majority of the men in town. "St. Marys stone was exported to other towns and cities. In 1851, 'cut stone fit for window sills and pilasters"...was being advertised in London at forty cents a foot delivered."[1]

The Lazier House

PRINCE EDWARD COUNTY

Nickolas Lazier was a prosperous mill owner who had come to Canada in 1802 after refusing to take the oath of allegiance to the American government. The Lazier family came to Upper Canada with much more than the average family. They had cash, livestock and owned slaves. He amassed a fortune in Canada from his milling operations.

Holmwood Farm
GLENGARRY COUNTY

Glengarry county was settled by people of Scottish descent. This prosperous farm was originally owned by the Cameron family. Carriages once travelled the path to this stately stone home which was built in 1854.

Cameron Hall (Holmwood Farm)   *Courtesy of Ontario Archives*

Forest Home

YORK COUNTY

The outstanding feature of this fieldstone house is its lovely trellised verandah. Marshall Macklin, the original owner of this home, was perhaps Upper Canada's first environmentalist. In an age when trees were often a nuisance, to be cleared as quickly as possible, Mr. Macklin saw the need to plant trees in order to preserve the topsoil.

Kirkmichael

WATERLOO COUNTY

William Dickson, a prominent lawyer, judge and member of the legislative council, built at least three houses in Upper Canada. "Kirkmichael" built in 1832, was the only one constructed in stone. Two of his other houses located in the Niagara area are recorded as being destroyed by the Americans during the War of 1812-1814. William Dickson is credited with being the founder of Galt (Cambridge, today) and "Kirkmichael" is located there.

Limestone Hall

HALTON COUNTY

John McGregor, the owner of this grand stone house, was a prosperous farmer with a large family. His father, Captain Peter McGregor, had served in the War of 1812 and was awarded a land grant for his service. The stone used in building the house was brought from a nearby quarry. A most experienced mason must have worked on the house or, at the very least supervised the stonework, as the building of Limestone Hall shows expertly dressed (smooth faced) stone walls. The stone for this house was said to have taken two years to prepare.

A stone' house, whether imposing like Limestone Hall or a cottage of simple proportions, said far better than words to the "folks back home" that their owners had met with success in Upper Canada.

"For stone is indeed the aristocrat of building materials."[2]

Footnotes

Chapter I

[1] Reaman, G. Elmore, *The Trail of the Black Walnut,* McClelland and Stewart 1957.
[2] Macrae, Marion. Adamson, Anthony, *The Ancestral Roof* Clarke, Irwin and Co. 1963.
[3] Ibid.
[4] Homewood Museum. "Homewood: Legacy of our Land"
[5] Archives of Ontario, RG 38. "Scrapbooks 1929-1939"

Chapter II

[1] Reaman, G. Elmore. *The Trail of the Black Walnut* Introduction xvii, McClelland and Stewart, 1957.
[2] Ibid, Introduction xvii
[3] Ibid, pg. 143
[4] John E. Brubacher Historical House, Self Guided Tour Pamphlet, 1983, pg 3
[5] Dunham, Mabel. *The Trail of The Conestoga* McClelland and Stewart, 1942.
[6] Reesor Genealogy, *The Reesor Family in Canada* privately published, 1980.

Chapter III

[1] Byers and McBurney, *The Governor's Road* University of Toronto Press 1982.

Chapter IV

[1] *Our Heritage in Stone* Heritage Cambridge 1978.
[2] Mr. Hugh Miller, owner of Thistle Ha' Farm, Claremont, Ontario.
[3] McCall-Newman, Christina. *Grits* McMillan of Canada.

Chapter V

[1] *Perth Remembered,* 1967.
[2] "The Old Scottish Architecture of Ontario" Cutts, Anson B. Canadian Geographical Journal, 1949. Vol. 38-39.

Chapter VI

[1] Ladell, John and Monica. *Inheritance* pg. 114-115, McMillan of Canada 1979.

Chapter VII

[1] Wilson, L.W., L.R. Pfaff *Early St. Marys* St. Marys-on-the-Thames Historical Society and The Boston Mills Press, Erin, 1981.
[2] Clifton-Taylor, ALec *The Pattern of English Building* Faber and Faber Ltd. London, England 1972.

Bibliography

Arthur, Eric *The Early Buildings of Ontario* University of Toronto Press, Toronto, 1938.

Bird, Michael, Kobayashi, Terry *A Splendid Harvest* Van Nostrand Reinhold, Toronto 1981.

Bruce, Harry, Harris, Chic. *A Basket of Apples* Oxford University Press. Toronto, 1982.

Byers and McBurney, Mary and Margaret *Rural Roots* University of Toronto Press, 1976.

Byers and McBurney, Mary and Margaret *Homesteads* University of Toronto Press, 1979.

Byers and McBurney, Mary and Margaret *The Governor's Road* University of Toronto Press 1982.

Dunham, Mabel. *The Trail of the Conestoga* McClelland and Stewart, Toronto, 1942.

Epp, Frank H. *Mennonites in Canada 1786-1920* MacMillan of Canada, Toronto, 1974.

Goddard, Jane Bennett, U.E. *Hans Waltimeyer* privately published, 1980.

Innis, Mary Quayle, edited by *Mrs. Simcoe's Diary* MacMillan of Canada, Toronto, 1965.

Harkness, John Graham, K.C. *A History of Stormont, Dundas and Glengarry* Mutual Press, Ottawa, 1946.

Hutchins, Nigel. *Restoring Old Houses* Van Nostrand Reinhold, Toronto, 1980.

Kauffman, Henry J. *The American Farmhouse* Hawthorne Books Inc. New York, 1975.

Ladell, John and Monica. *Inheritance* MacMillan of Canada, Toronto, 1979.

Macrae, Marion. Adamson, Anthony. *The Ancestral Roof* Clarke, Irwin and Co. Toronto, 1963.

Markham District Historical Society. *Markham 1793-1900* Hunter Rose, Toronto, 1979.

Ondjaatie and MacKenzie, Kim and Lois *Old Ontario Houses* Gage Publishing, Toronto, 1977.

Peacock, David and Suzanne. *Old Oakville* Heritage Press, Toronto.

Perth Remembered a collection of memories published for the Ontario Centennial, 1967.

Reaman, G. Elmore. *The Trail of the Black Walnut* McClelland and Stewart, Toronto, 1957.

Reid, C.S. Paddy. *Mansion in the Wilderness* Ministry of Culture and Recreation, Toronto, 1977.

Samuel, Alan E., Valerie Stevens, *Treasures of Canada* Samuel-Stevens, Toronto, 1980.

Schmidt, Carl F. *Cobblestone Masonry*

Wilson, L.W., L.R. Pfaff. *Early St. Marys* St. Marys on the Thames Historical Society and The Boston Mills Press, 1981.

Pamphlets

Historic Amherstburg, a Modern Town with Old World Charm.

Brubacher House, A Heritage House of Waterloo, 1983.

County Magazines, "The Magazine of Prince Edward County" publisher, Steve Campbell, Bloomfield Ontario.

Homewood: Legacy of our Land, a property of the Ontario Heritage Foundation, managed and operated by the Grenville Historical Society.

Huron County in Pioneer Times, James Scott, Huron County Historical Committee, 1954.

Hutchison House, owned and operated by the Peterborough Historical Society.

Kingston Walking Tour, Kingston and Area Real Estate Association.

Ontario: An Informal History of the Land and its People, Robert Choquette, Ministry of Education.

Our Heritage in Stone Heritage Cambridge, 1978.

Perth Walking Tour, Perth Chamber of Commerce.

Upper Canada Village, The St. Lawrence Parks Commission, Morrisburg.

Wentworth Bygones, The Head of the Lake Historical Society, Hamilton, 1977.

Wentworth Historical Society, Centennial Year, Hamilton, 1892.

Acknowledgments

We would like to thank Eugene Martel, archivist at the Ontario Archives, for his invaluable compiling of The Goulding Architectural Survey and Jean Leach for giving us access to the works of her late father, Eric Arthur. Museum curators, whether volunteer or professional, were a source of knowledge concerning their particular area. We would like to acknowledge the help of Barbara Sargeant in Prescott, Richard Schofield in Scarborough, John Lunau in Markham, Bob Wylie in Kingston, Joan Johnston in Williamstown and Barbara, at the Ontario Historical Society.

In Paris, Peter Vollmer and Marg Deans were most helpful as was Lynne Roelofson, in Cambridge. Prescott people deserving of special mention are Jack Morris, the Beaumonts and Bev Routledge. Prince Edward County had more than its share of resource people and Hal and Nan Roche were perhaps the first to help us with our book. Bob and Diana Grainger, Berva Howes, Marlene Campbell and Michelle Arsenault, all from The County, contributed to our research. George Edwin Carr, from St. Marys, June Carroll in Essex County and John Wright in Sault Ste Marie, each in their own way, assisted us.

The most thanks must go to the owners of these stone houses for their day to day loving care of our heritage.

R.M.
B.B.P.

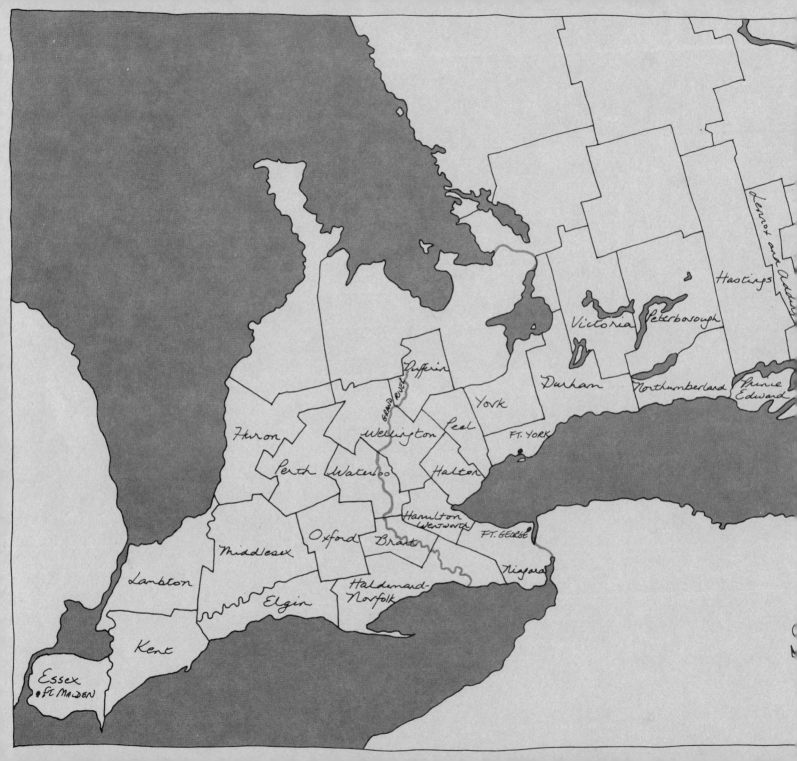